I Am Fabulous
The Journal

365 Days of Fabulous Inspirations

Trish M

Cover Design: Dream Design Concepts

Interior Design: Trish M Enterprises

Cover Photo Composite: 2B Photography

Editor: Trish M

ISBN-13 978-0-9897064-2-1

Dedication

To all the fabulous ladies who believe
that motivation and
inspiration is needed on a daily ba-
sis in order to be all that God has
destined them to be. May this book en-
courage you and help you on
your journey to greatness.

DAYS 1-30

Never stop believing.

NOTE TO SELF

Let your mind attract what you're thinking. Don't allow negative thoughts to get the best of you. So as a man thinketh, so is he. Guard your thought life. Great things shall manifest if only you can think it.

#IAmFabulous

Pressure is good. Stress is not.
Pressure makes diamonds.
Stress makes hospital bills.
Are you really ready to shine?
Don't run from the pressure.
Embrace it.

#IAmFabulous

Note To Self

Whenever God gets ready to do something major in your life, disruptions always come to hinder it! Know that they can't stop it, but they will try to delay it. Stay focused!

#IAmFabulous

NOTE TO SELF

The devil and his demons don't
have a problem with you
begging God for more things,
but they DO have a problem when
you are begging God for more of
HIM in your life. Are you looking
for more "things", or more of the
God Who can bring you the things?

#IAmFabulous

NOTE TO SELF

A successful life is a series of trade-offs. What are you willing to give up so that you can experience your next level of growth? #Selah

#IAmFabulous

NOTE TO SELF

If you aim at nothing, you'll hit it every time! Set your goals and GO AFTER THEM! What are your top priorities in this season of your life?

#IAmFabulous

Note To Self

You were born an original, created by God. Don't die being a duplicate of somebody else. God needs you to BE you, DO you and CELEBRATE you! How are you focusing on doing that in this season of your life?

#IAmFabulous

If you don't check your thoughts,
your thoughts will check you!
#MindControl

#IAmFabulous

NOTE TO SELF

NOTE TO SELF

Coming into your calling means
coming out of your comfort
zone. #Selah

#IAmFabulous

NOTE TO SELF

God allowed the mistake in
order to teach you a lesson.
#BeWise

#IAmFabulous

NOTE TO SELF

Being broke is a situation. Being
poor is a lifestyle. Your current
situation is not an indication of
your lifestyle. It's up to you to
change it. What are you doing to
change your situation so that
you can change your life?

#IAmFabulous

NOTE TO SELF

When you're married to excuses
and they won't let you be
GREAT....then it's time to file for
a DIVORCE!! If not, your
excuses will give you a life with
absolutely NOTHING being
produced from it! #Selah

#IAmFabulous

NOTE TO SELF

It's not how you start, it's how you finish. Don't quit. Keep pressing. Consistency is the key to your breakthrough!

#IAmFabulous

NOTE TO SELF

We cannot become who we want to be by remaining who we are. What does the "future you" look like?

#IAmFabulous

NOTE TO SELF

Life is like an elevator. On your way up, sometimes you have to stop and let some people off. Who is it that can't go to the top floor with you?

#IAmFabulous

Stop crossing oceans for people who won't even jump a puddle for you.

#IAmFabulous

NOTE TO SELF

NOTE TO SELF

Don't treat people as bad as they are. Treat them as good as you are, even when you don't believe they deserve it.

#IAmFabulous

NOTE TO SELF

Until you change your thinking,
you will always recycle your
experiences.

#IAmFabulous

NOTE TO SELF

Sometimes, instead of being in a season of breakthrough, God will put you in a season "going through". Be still and know that He is God.

#IAmFabulous

NOTE TO SELF

Don't ever let success get to
your head and never let failure
get to your heart. Stay humble
and keep moving.

#IAmFabulous

Note To Self

Do not let your NOW kill your
NEXT! Greater is at hand.
Just believe.

#IAmFabulous

NOTE TO SELF

Faith is like Wi-Fi, it's invisible
but it has the power to
connect you to what you need.
Remember that. How are you
missing your faith connection in
this season?

#IAmFabulous

Note To Self

God doesn't give you a dream
that matches your budget.
He's not checking your bank
account. He's checking your
faith account.

#IAmFabulous

NOTE TO SELF

People's words can't stop what
God has planned for you.
Let em talk...

#IAmFabulous

NOTE TO SELF

A strong woman accepts both
compliments & criticism
graciously knowing that it takes
both sun and rain for a flower to
come into bloom and grow.

#IAmFabulous

NOTE TO SELF

Don't say something permanently hurtful just because you're temporally upset.

#IAmFabulous

NOTE TO SELF

A scar shows you that you were stronger than whatever it was that tried to hurt you. Now carry on with your healing.

#IAmFabulous

NOTE TO SELF

Just because you're taking longer than others, doesn't mean that you're failing. Remember that.

#IAmFabulous

Note To Self

NOTE TO SELF

If you're not helping to make it right, then stop complaining about it being wrong. Do something about what you're complaining about.

#IAmFabulous

DAYS 31-60

Never stop the Process.

NOTE TO SELF

When God starts cutting things
and people away, that's when
you know you're getting closer
and closer to the promises that
He has for you.

#IAmFabulous

NOTE TO SELF

A comfort zone can be a beautiful place, but nothing ever grows there. So, step out of it.... NOW!

#IAmFabulous

NOTE TO SELF

Stop worrying about how it's
going to happen and start
trusting that it will happen!

#IAmFabulous

NOTE TO SELF

Half the battle is
refusing to QUIT!

#IAmFabulous

NOTE TO SELF

It's time to declutter your life.
Get rid of what you don't want
so you can make room for what
you DO want! #Selah

#IAmFabulous

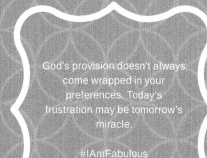

God's provision doesn't always come wrapped in your preferences. Today's frustration may be tomorrow's miracle.

#IAmFabulous

NOTE TO SELF

NOTE TO SELF

Most heroes wear a cape, but
ours wore a cross. He got you.
Remember that.

#IAmFabulous

NOTE TO SELF

God chose you. Not because of
who you are, but because of
what you can become. You are
His POTENTIAL. Now walk in
your GREATNESS!

#IAmFabulous

NOTE TO SELF

You only live once, but if you do
it right, once is enough.
What do you need to make
sure you do well at?

#IAmFabulous

NOTE TO SELF

The symptoms of smallmindedness
are gossip, offense and drama.
People on a path of purpose don't
have time for that.

#IAmFabulous

NOTE TO SELF

Don't let fear decide your future.

#IAmFabulous

NOTE TO SELF

You're not born with confidence.
You build it.

#IAmFabulous

NOTE TO SELF

Ask yourself if what you are
doing today is getting you closer
to where you want to be
tomorrow. Is there anything
that you need to change?

#IAmFabulous

NOTE TO SELF

If you cannot do great things,
do small things in a great way.

#IAmFabulous

NOTE TO SELF

Focus on the solution...
not the problem.

#IAmFabulous

NOTE TO SELF

Don't be so consumed with winning that you fail to realize that you already are in some area of your life.

#IAmFabulous

Note To Self

NOTE TO SELF

Don't add people to your life
with the same characteristics as
the people you asked God to
remove.

#IAmFabulous

Note To Self

Blessings can be right around the corner, but if you never leave the block...you'll miss it.

#IAmFabulous

NOTE TO SELF

When FAVOR is on you, no matter what you are thrown in, you'll always rise to the top. You got FAVOR. Remember that.

#IAmFabulous

NOTE TO SELF

The blessed don't beef with the miserable.

#IAmFabulous

NOTE TO SELF

A strong woman looks a challenge dead in the eye and gives it a wink letting it know....
I GOT YOU!

#IAmFabulous

NOTE TO SELF

Your current situation is not
your final destination.

#IAmFabulous

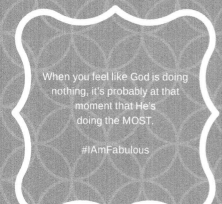

NOTE TO SELF

When you feel like God is doing nothing, it's probably at that moment that He's doing the MOST.

#IAmFabulous

NOTE TO SELF

The best revenge is happiness.
Nothing drives people more
crazy than seeing someone
actually having a good life.

#IAmFabulous

NOTE TO SELF

Be aware of open doors.
Sometimes there will
something
in front of it to test you before
you walk through.

#IAmFabulous

NOTE TO SELF

Don't let depression come in
due to a temporary situation.

#IAmFabulous

The first to apologize is the bravest. The first to forgive is the strongest. The first to forget is the happiest.

#IAmFabulous

NOTE TO SELF

NOTE TO SELF

Sometimes you have to ask
yourself if you're being led by
the Spirit or by your wound.

#IAmFabulous

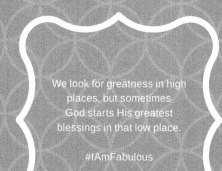

We look for greatness in high places, but sometimes God starts His greatest blessings in that low place.

#IAmFabulous

NOTE TO SELF

DAYS 61-90

Never stop existing.

NOTE TO SELF

There are 7 days in a week. Someday isn't one of them. If not now...when?? Whatever God put in your spirit to do.... DO IT! Delayed obedience is still disobedience.

#IAmFabulous

NOTE TO SELF

If you don't like something, then take away it's only power....YOUR ATTENTION. Whatis it that you are wasting your time giving attention to? #Selah

#IAmFabulous

NOTE TO SELF

You have been assigned to this
mountain to show others it
can be moved.

#IAmFabulous

Knowledge is knowing what
to say. Wisdom is knowing
when to say it.

#IAmFabulous

Note To Self

You will always travel in the
direction of your thinking.

#IAmFabulous

NOTE TO SELF

You don't have to rebuild a
relationship with everyone
you've forgiven.

#IAmFabulous

NOTE TO SELF

Speak in such a way that
others love to listen to you.
Listen in such a way that
others love to speak to you.

#IAmFabulous

NOTE TO SELF

The most valuable thing you can make is a mistake. You can't learn anything from being perfect.

#IAmFabulous

Note To Self

Surround yourself with
people who talk about
visions and ideas, not other
people.

#IAmFabulous

NOTE TO SELF

Do not get upset with people or situations. Both are powerless without your reaction.

#IAmFabulous

Note To Self

Don't let the little things
steal your happiness.

#IAmFabulous

NOTE TO SELF

If you want to fly, give up the things that weigh you down.

#IAmFabulous

NOTE TO SELF

When you forgive, you heal.
When you let go, you grow.

#IAmFabulous

Note To Self

You gotta stop watering dead plants. Move on please.

#IAmFabulous

NOTE TO SELF

If your presence doesn't add
value, your absence won't
make a difference.

#IAmFabulous

NOTE TO SELF

People do not decide their future. They decide their habits and their habits decide their future.

#IAmFabulous

NOTE TO SELF

Difficult roads lead to
beautiful destinations.

#IAmFabulous

NOTE TO SELF

Be determined to stay in a place called "Negativity Not Welcomed". #Selah

#IAmFabulous

NOTE TO SELF

If you want greatness, then
don't complain about being
stretched. Great things
happen when you come out of
your comfort zone.

#IAmFabulous

NOTE TO SELF

Don't worry. They are
following you even when
they act like they're not. Be
the light that shines even
before those that left you.

#IAmFabulous

Note To Self

NOTE TO SELF

Forget the mistake, but let
the lesson never be
forgotten.

#IAmFabulous

Note To Self

Don't rip yourself to pieces just so you can make others whole. People can burn you out, but God wants you to be WHOLE. #Selah

#IAmFabulous

NOTE TO SELF

When you fall down, embrace that moment. There's something in that place that you fell that you are suppose to find. Remember that.

#IAmFabulous

NOTE TO SELF

Old keys won't open new
doors. Move on.

#IAmFabulous

NOTE TO SELF

Don't show up to every
argument that you're invited
to. It's ok to miss a party.
#Selah

#IAmFabulous

Note To Self

NOTE TO SELF

Let your mind attract what you're thinking. Watch your thoughts. #Selah

#IAmFabulous

NOTE TO SELF

It doesn't matter who you used to be. What matters is who you're willing to become.

#IAmFabulous

NOTE TO SELF

The reason people resist change is because they focus on what they have to give up instead of what they have to gain.

#IAmFabulous

DAYS 91-120

Never stop winning.

NOTE TO SELF

A woman's heart should be
so hidden in God that a man
has to seek Him just to
find her.

#IAmFabulous

Note To Self

If you can't handle being
talked about, then you're
not ready for success.

#IAmFabulous

NOTE TO SELF

If you're not making mistakes,
you're not learning.

#IAmFabulous

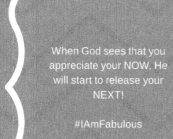

When God sees that you
appreciate your NOW, He
will start to release your
NEXT!

#IAmFabulous

NOTE TO SELF

NOTE TO SELF

The struggle you're in today is developing the strength you need for tomorrow.

#IAmFabulous

NOTE TO SELF

You can't have a million
dollar dream with a
minimum wage work ethic.

#IAmFabulous

NOTE TO SELF

Sometimes people can't apologize because they're ashamed. Forgive them anyway!

#IAmFabulous

NOTE TO SELF

Be so positive that negative
people don't want to be
around you.

#IAmFabulous

NOTE TO SELF

When the wrong people leave,
they just shifted your
atmosphere for the right
things to start happening.
Embrace the shift! #Selah

#IAmFabulous

NOTE TO SELF

Sometimes you have to be OK with a "sorry" that you never got.

#IAmFabulous

NOTE TO SELF

God heard you the first time.
Be patient.

#IAmFabulous

NOTE TO SELF

Don't be so afraid of failure
that you can't get to success.

#IAmFabulous

NOTE TO SELF

Sometimes God will change
your circle so that He can
change your life! Embrace it!

#IAmFabulous

NOTE TO SELF

When God gives you the sign
that you asked for, don't
ignore it!

#IAmFabulous

NOTE TO SELF

You're not born just to pay
bills and die. Remember that.

#IAmFabulous

Note To Self

Don't go back to less just
because you're too impatient
to wait for God's best.

#IAmFabulous

Note To Self

Sometimes God will give you
exactly what you wanted just
to show you it's not what you
needed.

#IAmFabulous

NOTE TO SELF

Not everything that is faced
can be changed, but nothing
can be changed until
it is faced.

#IAmFabulous

NOTE TO SELF

If you don't fight for what you
want, don't cry for
what you lost.

#IAmFabulous

NOTE TO SELF

Forget the pains of the past
and enjoy the blessings of
your present.

#IAmFabulous

Note To Self

If you can't control your
mouth, you will have a hard
time controlling your life.

#IAmFabulous

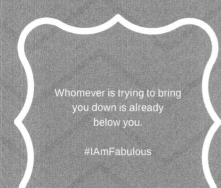

Whomever is trying to bring you down is already below you.

#IAmFabulous

NOTE TO SELF

NOTE TO SELF

Stop talking yourself out of
your blessings.

#IAmFabulous

NOTE TO SELF

Be willing to work for everything that you prayed for.

#IAmFabulous

NOTE TO SELF

Don't let the enemy believe in your potential more than you do. That's why he's trying to stop you! Don't fall for it!

#IAmFabulous

NOTE TO SELF

- I'm gonna
make you proud!

#IAmFabulous

NOTE TO SELF

Anger is energy. Focus it and
direct it towards your true
adversary, Satan, instead
of the ones you love.

#IAmFabulous

NOTE TO SELF

Your greatest fear should not be of failure, but of succeeding at something that doesn't even matter.

#IAmFabulous

NOTE TO SELF

Don't fret. When things seem
like they're falling apart they
just might actually be
falling into place.

#IAmFabulous

NOTE TO SELF

Don't let the person who can't see your worth end up being YOU.

#IAmFabulous

DAYS 121-150

Never stop declaring.

NOTE TO SELF

When you align yourself with people who should be a part of your HISTORY and not your DESTINY, then you're missing God.

#IAmFabulous

Note To Self

There are 2 types of pain: one that HURTS you and the other that CHANGES you. Embrace them both.

#IAmFabulous

NOTE TO SELF

When you know who you are
now and understand who you
used to be then, you have NO
time to respond to folks who try
to put you back in "USE TO"
mode!

#IAmFabulous

NOTE TO SELF

Don't expect people to
understand your GRIND when
God didn't give them your
VISION.

#IAmFabulous

NOTE TO SELF

Don't ruin a good TODAY by
thinking about a bad
yesterday. When it's time to let
it go, just let it go.

#IAmFabulous

NOTE TO SELF

Though they see you struggle,
never let them see you quit.

#IAmFabulous

NOTE TO SELF

Don't rationalize yourself out
of the will of God. You are in a
season of great faith. Everything
won't make sense.
Remember that

#IAmFabulous

NOTE TO SELF

God never told you to
impress people. He told you to
love them. #Selah

#IAmFabulous

NOTE TO SELF

Even though you're
emotionally tired....keep going.

#IAmFabulous

NOTE TO SELF

You step out on faith while your critics sit on the boat. Let them talk as you pass them by.
#ByeFelicia

#IAmFabulous

NOTE TO SELF

You've been saved from your
past. Remember that.

#IAmFabulous

NOTE TO SELF

The less you respond to negative people, the more peaceful you'll be.

#IAmFabulous

NOTE TO SELF

If serving others is beneath you, then leading is beyond you.

#IAmFabulous

Note To Self

Your mind will believe whatever you tell it. Evaluate what you're putting in your mind. Feed it faith. Feed it truth. Feed it empowerment. Greater is waiting. It's time for your mind to believe it.

#IAmFabulous

NOTE TO SELF

_____
_____
_____
_____
_____
_____
_____
_____
_____

You can't spell the word
"challenge" without including
the word "change". If you're
ready for a change, then
challenge yourself to do
somethings differently. If it
doesn't challenge you, it won't
change you.

#IAmFabulous

NOTE TO SELF

You did not wake up today to
be mediocre. Greatness
awaits! Now act like it!

#IAmFabulous

NOTE TO SELF

Stop giving the devil access
to your life. That's all.

#IAmFabulous

NOTE TO SELF

Are you always the smartest
person in the room?
Evaluate your
connections daily.

#IAmFabulous

NOTE TO SELF

Don't cry about having a lot on your plate when your goal was to eat. #Selah

#IAmFabulous

NOTE TO SELF

Prayer changes things.
After you pray, give it to God,
and trust that He can
handle it. Not you.

#IAmFabulous

Note To Self

If you're focused on being who you're destined to be, why hang around folk who's showing signs of jealousy before you even get to that destined place? #Selah

#IAmFabulous

A negative mind will never
give you a positive life.

#IAmFabulous

NOTE TO SELF

Can you handle the process
that it takes to get to the
promise? If so, keep it
moving- you'll get there.

#IAmFabulous

Note To Self

You are what you do, not
what you say you'll do.

#IAmFabulous

NOTE TO SELF

You are what you do, not
what you say you'll do.

#IAmFabulous

NOTE TO SELF

"Blessed is she who has
believed that the Lord would
fulfill his promises to her!"
Luke 1:45

#IAmFabulous

NOTE TO SELF

"She BELIEVED she COULD,
so she DID"

#IAmFabulous

NOTE TO SELF

Worry Ends where
Faith Begins.

#IAmFabulous

NOTE TO SELF

When you know yourself,
you are empowered. When
you accept yourself, you are
invincible.

#IAmFabulous

NOTE TO SELF

Be strong when you are weak.
Be brave when you are scared.
Be humble when you are
victorious.

#IAmFabulous

DAYS 151-180

Never stop dreaming.

Note To Self

NOTE TO SELF

Every king was once a crying
baby and every building was
once a picture. Its not about
where you are today but
where you will
reach tomorrow.

#IAMFabulous

NOTE TO SELF

NOTE TO SELF

NOTE TO SELF

Note To Self

Every Accomplishment
begins with the decision to try.

#IAmFabulous

NOTE TO SELF

He who kneels before God
can stand before anyone

#IAmFabulous

What techniques have I put
in place in the already started
declutter to maintain a
minimalist life?

What's working?

NOTE TO SELF

Happiness is a journey,
Not a destination

#IAmFabulous

NOTE TO SELF

Note To Self

NOTE TO SELF

"Whatever the mind of man can conceive and believe it can achieve" ~Napoleon Hill

#IAmFabulous

NOTE TO SELF

NOTE TO SELF

A smooth sea never made a
skillful sailor.

#IAmFabulous

Note To Self

NOTE TO SELF

NOTE TO SELF

Life is not about waiting for
the storm to pass, it's about
learning how to dance in
the rain.

#IAmFabulous

NOTE TO SELF

Note To Self

NOTE TO SELF

The only person you should
try to be better than is the
person you were yesterday.

#IAmFabulous

NOTE TO SELF

DAYS 181-210

Never stop pursuing.

NOTE TO SELF

It is not our abilities but
persistence that ultimately
leads us to our greatest
achievements.

#IAmFabulous

NOTE TO SELF

Don't end up regretting the
things you didn't do when you
had the chance.

#IAmFabulous

Note To Self

In order to succeed, your
desire for success should be
greater than your fear of failure.

#IAmFabulous

Go where you are celebrated –
not tolerated. If they can't
see the real value of you, it's time
for a new start. Move on.

#IAmFabulous

NOTE TO SELF

Don't be afraid to stand for
what you believe in, even if
that means standing alone.

#IAmFabulous

Success seems to be
connected with action.
Successful people keep moving.
They make mistakes, but they
don't quit.

#IAmFabulous

Note To Self

Make today as FABULOUS
as you can.

#IAmFabulous

Note To Self

Things work out best for those
who make the best of how
things work out.

#IAmFabulous

NOTE TO SELF

Courage doesn't always roar.
Sometimes courage is the
quiet voice at the end of the day
saying," I will try again
tomorrow".

#IAmFabulous

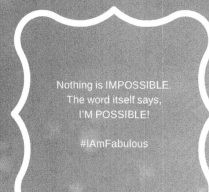

Nothing is IMPOSSIBLE.
The word itself says,
I'M POSSIBLE!

#IAmFabulous

NOTE TO SELF

NOTE TO SELF

Abundance is not something we acquire. It is something we tune into.

#IAmFabulous

Philippians 4:13
I can do all things through him
who strengthens me.

#IAmFabulous

NOTE TO SELF

Isaiah 41:10
Fear not, for I am with you; be
not dismayed, for I am your
God; I will strengthen you, I will
help you, I will uphold you
with my righteous right hand.

#IAmFabulous

NOTE TO SELF

Proverbs 3:5-5
Trust in the LORD with all
your heart, and do not lean on
your own understanding. 6 In
all your ways acknowledge
him, and he will make straight
your paths.

#IAmFabulous

NOTE TO SELF

Deuteronomy 31:6
Be strong and courageous. Do
not fear or be in dread of them,
for it is the LORD your God who
goes with you. He will not
leave you or forsake you."

#IAmFabulous

NOTE TO SELF

Galatians 5:22-23
But the fruit of the Spirit is
love, joy, peace, patience,
kindness, goodness,
faithfulness, gentleness, selfcontrol;
against such things there is
no law.

#IAmFabulous

NOTE TO SELF

Romans 8:28
And we know that for those who
love God, all things work together for good, for those who are called according to his purpose.

#IAmFabulous

NOTE TO SELF

Jeremiah 29:11
For I know the plans I have for
you, declares the LORD, plans
for welfare and not for evil, to
give you a future and a hope.

#IAmFabulous

NOTE TO SELF

Romans 12:12
Rejoice in hope, be patient in
tribulation, be constant
in prayer.

#IAmFabulous

Galatians 6:9
And let us not grow weary of
doing good, for in due season
we will reap, if we do
not give up.

#IAmFabulous

NOTE TO SELF

2 Timothy 1:7
For God gave us a spirit not
of fear but of power and love
and
a strong mind.

#IAmFabulous

NOTE TO SELF

Isaiah 40:31
but they who wait for the
LORD shall renew their
strength; they shall mount up
with wings like eagles; they
shall run and not be weary;
they shall walk and not faint.

#IAmFabulous

NOTE TO SELF

Psalms 23:4
Even though I walk through
the valley of the shadow of
death, I will fear no evil, for
you are with me; your rod and
your staff, they comfort me.

#IAmFabulous

NOTE TO SELF

Psalms 37:4
Delight yourself in the LORD,
and he will give you the
desires of your heart.

#IAmFabulous

NOTE TO SELF

Strive not to be a success, but
rather to be of value.
–Albert Einstein

#IAmFabulous

NOTE TO SELF

Life is 10% what happens to you, and 90% of how you react to it.

#IAmFabulous

NOTE TO SELF

Either you run the day, or the
day runs you. –Jim Rohn

#IAmFabulous

NOTE TO SELF

Whether you think you can or
you think you can't, you're
right. It's all in what
you believe.

#IAmFabulous

NOTE TO SELF

The two most important days
in your life are the day you
are born and the day you find
out why. —Mark Twain

#IAmFabulous

People often say that motivation doesn't last. Well, neither does bathing. That's why we recommend it daily.
—Zig Ziglar

#IAmFabulous

DAYS 211-240

Never stop fighting.

NOTE TO SELF

Every day is a new beginning.
Smile. Try again. The key is to
not give up.

#IAmFabulous

NOTE TO SELF

You are strong because you had moments of weakness. They helped strengthen your walk day by day. Don't give up.

#IAmFabulous

NOTE TO SELF

You are fearless because you
have been afraid. You've
learned to do life scared.
That's how you overcome the
fears of life. You simply do it.
Fear will not hold
you back.

#IAmFabulous

NOTE TO SELF

You are wise because you've been foolish. Mistakes don't control you. You learn from them and keep it moving.

#IAmFabulous

NOTE TO SELF

Fall asleep with a dream, but
wake up with a purpose.

#IAmFabulous

NOTE TO SELF

A river cuts through a rock not because of its power, but because of its persistence. You are that river. Flow. Don't quit.

#IAmFabulous

NOTE TO SELF

It's a slow process, but
quitting won't speed it up.

#IAmFabulous

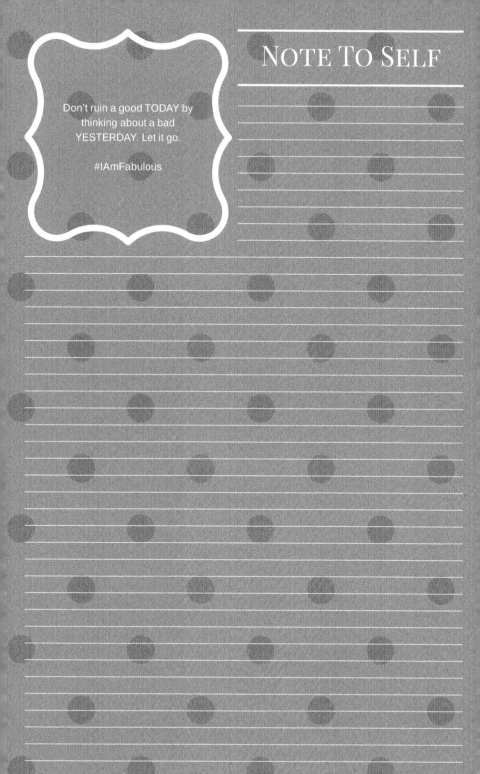

NOTE TO SELF

Don't ruin a good TODAY by
thinking about a bad
YESTERDAY. Let it go.

#IAmFabulous

NOTE TO SELF

When you start seeing your
worth, you'll find it harder to
stay around people who don't.

#IAmFabulous

NOTE TO SELF

You can never cross the ocean until you have enough courage to lose sight of the shore.

#IAmFabulous

Note To Self

Being positive in a negative situation is not being naive. It's called being a leader.

#IAmFabulous

NOTE TO SELF

Sometimes it takes having an overwhelming breakdown in order to have an undeniable breakthrough.

#IAmFabulous

NOTE TO SELF

You were given this life
because you are strong
enough to live it.

#IAmFabulous

NOTE TO SELF

Make yourself a priority.

#IAmFabulous

Note To Self

Never apologize for having
high standards.

#IAmFabulous

NOTE TO SELF

Making a big life change is
pretty scary. What's even
scarier is regretting that you
never did.

#IAmFabulous

NOTE TO SELF

No one can make you feel
worthless without your
consent. You have the power
to get rid of the negativity,
but will you?

#IAmFabulous

Doubts kill more dreams than
failure ever will.

#IAmFabulous

NOTE TO SELF

To make a difference in someone's life, you don't have to be brillant, rich or even a millionaire. You just simply have to care.

#IAmFabulous

Note To Self

You must do the thing which
you think you cannot do.
Prove yourself wrong.

#IAmFabulous

Note To Self

Everything comes to you at
the right moment. Be patient.

#IAmFabulous

NOTE TO SELF

Be the person you want to
have in YOUR life.

#IAmFabulous

Note To Self

Let go of what's already
GONE.

#IAmFabulous

NOTE TO SELF

The secret of your future is hidden in your daily routine. What are you doing? #Selah

#IAmFabulous

Note To Self

Everything you go through
will grow you if you let it.

#IAmFabulous

NOTE TO SELF

There's a way to do it better-
FIND IT.

#IAmFabulous

NOTE TO SELF

If someone treats you like
an option, leave them like a
CHOICE.

#IAmFabulous

NOTE TO SELF

Don't be stuck in a place that
you don't belong. Leave.

#IAmFabulous

DAYS 241-270

Never stop praying.

NOTE TO SELF

Sometimes God will give you
exactly what you wanted only
to show you it's not what you
needed.

#IAmFabulous

NOTE TO SELF

Don't go back to less just
because you're too impatient
to wait for God's best!

#IAmFabulous

_____
_____
_____
_____
_____
_____
_____
_____
_____
_____
_____
_____
_____
_____
_____
_____
_____
_____
_____
_____
_____
_____
_____
_____
_____
_____
_____

NOTE TO SELF

There's more to your life
than just paying bills
and dying.

#IAmFabulous

When God gives you the sign
that you asked for, don't
ignore it.

#IAmFabulous

NOTE TO SELF

NOTE TO SELF

Sometimes God will change
your circle so that He can
change your life. Embrace it!

#IAmFabulous

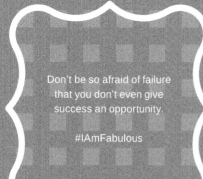

Don't be so afraid of failure
that you don't even give
success an opportunity.

#IAmFabulous

NOTE TO SELF

NOTE TO SELF

God heard you.
Be patient.

#IAmFabulous

Sometimes you have to be ok with a "sorry" that you NEVER got.

#IAmFabulous

Note To Self

NOTE TO SELF

When the wrong people
leave, they just opened up the
door for the right things to start
happening in your life.

#IAmFabulous

NOTE TO SELF

Be so positive and energetic
that negative people don't
want to be around you.

#IAmFabulous

NOTE TO SELF

Sometimes people can't apologize because they're ashamed. Forgive them anyway.

#IAmFabulous

You can have a million dollar
dream with a minimum wage
work ethic. Don't let that be you.
Work hard for what you want.

#IAmFabulous

NOTE TO SELF

The struggle you're in today
is developing the strength
that you need for tomorrow.

#IAmFabulous

NOTE TO SELF

When God sees that you
appreciate your NOW, He'll
begin to release you into
your NEXT.

#IAmFabulous

NOTE TO SELF

If you're not making
mistakes, you're not learning.

#IAmFabulous

NOTE TO SELF

Don't get confused with what's happening around you. It may not look like it or seem like it, but know that God is up to something BIG on your behalf! Do you not perceive it?

#IAmFabulous

NOTE TO SELF

If you can't handle being talked
about, then you're not
ready for success.

#IAmFabulous

NOTE TO SELF

Don't allow your fears to cancel out what God is trying to do in your life. Your next level requires FAITH, not fear. Fear cancels out faith! Do it scared! Scared and all...Just do it!! Remember that!

#IAmFabulous

Note To Self

That setback that just
happened is only allowing
you to be set right back up to
your rightful position and place.

#IAmFabulous

NOTE TO SELF

When you don't know what else to do....pray and simply trust God. I know it may be a challenge. I know it may seem pointless. It may even seem stupid, but in the midst of adversity, talk to God and remember that He hears you. He is able to meet you at your point of need. Just trust Him.

#IAmFabulous

NOTE TO SELF

Let your mind attract what you are thinking. Watch your thoughts.

#IAmFabulous

NOTE TO SELF

Don't let the attitude of others dictate yours. When they come against you, cuss you out, lie on you, reject you, hate you, etc....you LOVE anyway. Confuse them and the enemy that's using them by simply showing LOVE! Let that be your ONLY "getback". #Love

#IAmFabulous

Note To Self

You might can't see it, but you sure can say it! Don't be afraid to speak life into your atmosphere of chaos. You have power in your tongue! Are you speaking fruitful or unfruitful things? Check yourself. When your thoughts and words change, your entire life can change as well!

#IAmFabulous

NOTE TO SELF

Don't show up to every argument that you are invited to. It's ok to miss a party. #Selah

#IAmFabulous

NOTE TO SELF

Old keys don't open new doors.
Move On.

#IAmFabulous

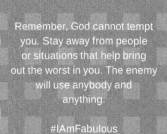

NOTE TO SELF

Remember, God cannot tempt
you. Stay away from people
or situations that help bring
out the worst in you. The enemy
will use anybody and
anything.

#IAmFabulous

NOTE TO SELF

Be determined to stay in a
place called "Negativity NOT
welcomed here".

#IAmFabulous

When you fall down, embrace
that moment. There's something
in that "fall" that you're suppose
to find. Grow from it.

#IAmFabulous

NOTE TO SELF

DAYS 271-300

Never stop planning.

Note To Self

There's something in you
that's telling you...YOU CAN'T
GIVE UP! You are an
overcomer. You got this.
When God's word tells you that
you are more than a conqueror
through Him.....it's time you
started believing it!

#IAmFabulous

NOTE TO SELF

Don't rip yourself to pieces just
so you can make others whole.
People can burn you out, but
God needs you to be WHOLE.

#IAmFabulous

Note To Self

You think you're down now, but do you see what I see? God has a comeback spirit deep down on the inside of you that has been lying dormant. But the Lord is saying...you are about to RISE up like never before and cross the Red Sea!

#IAmFabulous

NOTE TO SELF

Forget the mistake, but let the
lesson never be forgotten.

#IAmFabulous

NOTE TO SELF

You're the one person that can change your life. God has given you that authority; now use it.

#IAmFabulous

NOTE TO SELF

If you can't control your mouth,
you'll have a hard time
controlling your life.

#IAmFabulous

NOTE TO SELF

Stop watering seeds that should NOT be watered. They're only producing weeds in your life. When you cast your pearls to the swine, they'll only trample over them and not appreciate them. Your pearls are valuable. Your seed is valuable. YOU have to be the one to believe it.

#IAmFabulous

NOTE TO SELF

Be aware of open doors.
Sometimes there will be
something in front of it to test
you before you walk through it.

#IAmFabulous

Note To Self

NOTE TO SELF

When you feel like God is doing NOTHING, it's probably at that moment that He's doing the MOST. You have no clue!

#IAmFabulous

NOTE TO SELF

Your current situation is not
your final destination.

#IAmFabulous

NOTE TO SELF

A strong woman looks a
challenge dead in the eye and
gives it a wink letting it know...
I GOT YOU!

#IAmFabulous

NOTE TO SELF

The blessed don't beef with the MISERABLE.

#IAmFabulous

When you got favor, you'll
always rise to the top!

#IAmFabulous

NOTE TO SELF

Blessings can be right around
the corner, but if you never
leave the block, you'll miss it!

#IAmFabulous

NOTE TO SELF

Don't add people to your life with the same characteristics as the people you asked God to remove.

#IAmFabulous

Note To Self

NOTE TO SELF

Destiny called and said you need
to make some changes in order for
you to get to your next level.

#IAmFabulous

NOTE TO SELF

Don't ask what the meaning of life is. You define it.

#IAmFabulous

NOTE TO SELF

Don't be so consumed in winning that you fail to realize that you already are in some area of your life.

#IAmFabulous

NOTE TO SELF

Focus on the solution...not the problem.

#IAmFabulous

NOTE TO SELF

If you cannot do great things,
do small things in a great way.

#IAmFabulous

NOTE TO SELF

Ask yourself if what you are
doing today is getting you closer
to where you want to be tomorrow.

#IAmFabulous

Note To Self

You're not born with confidence.
You build it.

#IAmFabulous

Note To Self

Don't let fear decide your future.

#IAmFabulous

NOTE TO SELF

The symptoms of small-mindedness are gossip, offense and drama. People on a path to purpose don't have time for that.

#IAmFabulous

NOTE TO SELF

You only live once, but if you do
it right, once is all you need.

#IAmFabulous

NOTE TO SELF

God chose you not because of
who you are, but because of who
you can become. You are His
POTENTIAL. Now walk in your
GREATNESS!

#IAmFabulous

NOTE TO SELF

Most heroes wear a cape, but
ours wore a cross. He got you.
Remember that.

#IAmFabulous

NOTE TO SELF

God's provision doesn't always
come wrapped in your
preferences. Today's frustration
may be tomorrow's miracle.

#IAmFabulous

DAYS 301-330

Never stop trusting God.

NOTE TO SELF

It's time to declutter your life.
Get rid of what you don't want
so that you can make room for
what you DO want.

#IAmFabulous

Half the battle is refusing to QUIT!!

#IAmFabulous

NOTE TO SELF

NOTE TO SELF

Stop worrying about how it's
going to happen and start
trusting that it WILL happen.

#IAmFabulous

NOTE TO SELF

A comfort zone is a beautiful place, but nothing ever grows there. So step out of it...NOW!

#IAmFabulous

NOTE TO SELF

When God starts cutting
things and people away, that's
when you know you're getting
closer and closer to the
promises that He has for you.

#IAmFabulous

NOTE TO SELF

It's great to be inspired by someone, but you should never want to be that person. Use that inspiration to get to the next level of being YOU.

#IAmFabulous

NOTE TO SELF

If you're not helping to make
it right, then stop complaining
about it being wrong.

#IAmFabulous

NOTE TO SELF

A vision without action is a daydream. Action without vision is a nightmare.

#IAmFabulous

NOTE TO SELF

Just because you're taking
longer than others, doesn't
mean that you're failing.
Remember that.

#IAmFabulous

NOTE TO SELF

A scar shows you that you
were stronger than whatever it
was that tried to hurt you. Now
carry on with your healing.

#IAmFabulous

NOTE TO SELF

Don't say something that's permanently hurtful just because you're temporarily upset.

#IAmFabulous

NOTE TO SELF

A strong woman takes compliments and criticism graciously knowing that it takes sun and rain for a flower to bloom and grow.

#IAmFabulous

NOTE TO SELF

People's words can't stop
what God has planned for you.
Let them talk.

#IAmFabulous

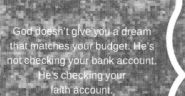

NOTE TO SELF

God doesn't give you a dream
that matches your budget. He's
not checking your bank account.
He's checking your
faith account.

#IAmFabulous

NOTE TO SELF

Faith is like Wi-Fi. It's
invisible, but it has the power
to connect you to what you need.
Remember that.

#IAmFabulous

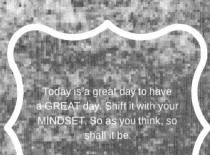

Today is a great day to have a GREAT day. Shift it with your MINDSET. So as you think, so shall it be.

#IAmFabulous

NOTE TO SELF

NOTE TO SELF

Do not let your NOW kill your NEXT! Greater is at hand. Just BELIEVE.

#IAmFabulous

Note To Self

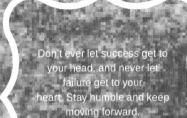

Don't ever let success get to
your head, and never let
failure get to your
heart. Stay humble and keep
moving forward.

#IAmFabulous

NOTE TO SELF

Sometimes instead of being in a season of BREAKTHROUGH, God will have you in a season of GOING THROUGH. Be still and know that He is God.

#IAmFabulous

Until you change your thinking, you'll always recycle your experiences.

#IAmFabulous

NOTE TO SELF

NOTE TO SELF

Stop crossing oceans for
people who won't even jump a
puddle for you.

#IAmFabulous

NOTE TO SELF

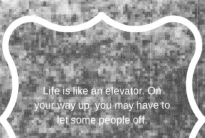

Life is like an elevator. On your way up, you may have to let some people off.

#IAmFabulous

NOTE TO SELF

Don't treat people as bad as
they are. Treat them as good
as you are.

#IAmFabulous

NOTE TO SELF

We cannot become who we
want to be by remaining who
we are.

#IAmFabulous

NOTE TO SELF

Be willing to work for
everything that you prayed for.

#IAmFabulous

NOTE TO SELF

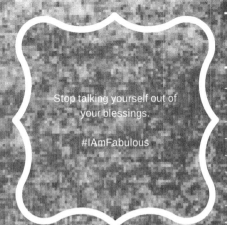

Stop talking yourself out of
your blessings.

#IAmFabulous

NOTE TO SELF

Don't let the person who can't
see your worth end up being
YOU.

#IAmFabulous

Don't fret. When things seem like they're falling apart, they actually might just be falling into place.

#IAmFabulous

NOTE TO SELF

NOTE TO SELF

Can you handle the process
that it takes to get to the
promise? If so....keep moving.

#IAmFabulous

NOTE TO SELF

You are in a season where you truly have to have that "walking on the water" faith. God is taking you to a new place and doing a new thing in this season. Are you ready?

#IAmFabulous

DAYS 331-365

Never stop believing.

NOTE TO SELF

A dream written down with a
date becomes a GOAL A goal
broken down into steps
becomes a PLAN. A plan
backed by ACTION makes your
dream a REALITY.

#IAmFabulous

NOTE TO SELF

If your goals set you apart
from the crowd, then don't
be afraid to stand alone.

#IAmFabulous

NOTE TO SELF

Set a goal that makes you want
to jump out of bed in the
morning.

#IAmFabulous

Winners are losers who got
up and gave it another try.

#IAmFabulous

NOTE TO SELF

Don't wait for the opportunity.
Create it.

#IAmFabulous

NOTE TO SELF

Do what you HAVE to do until you can do what you WANT to do.

#IAmFabulous

NOTE TO SELF

It doesn't matter how slow you're going as long as you don't stop.

#IAmFabulous

NOTE TO SELF

Take control of your finances. Sacrifice until you come into your steak and potato season.

#IAmFabulous

NOTE TO SELF

Even if you're on the right track, you'll get run over if you just sit there.

#IAmFabulous

NOTE TO SELF

Nothing will work unless you do.

#IAmFabulous

Note To Self

It's never too late to get it together.

#IAmFabulous

NOTE TO SELF

Be stronger than your excuses.

#IAmFabulous

Note To Self

You don't need anyone's
permission to be GREAT.

#IAmFabulous

NOTE TO SELF

It's better to be hurt by the truth
than comforted with a lie.

#IAmFabulous

NOTE TO SELF

If you don't take the time to
design and plan your life, then
you'll have to settle for what
life gives you.

#IAmFabulous

NOTE TO SELF

Eliminate what doesn't help you evolve.

#IAmFabulous

Note To Self

NOTE TO SELF

The devil loves it when you
WORRY about what's next
because he knows you're not
enjoying nor embracing
what God is doing in
your NOW!

#IAmFabulous

NOTE TO SELF

Everything that you want is
on the other side of what you
have been afraid of doing.

#IAmFabulous

NOTE TO SELF

Staying offended is like
drinking poison and hoping
that it teaches the other person
a lesson.

#IAmFabulous

NOTE TO SELF

Not being where you want to
be in life is ok. Doing nothing
about it is where the problem
comes in.

#IAmFabulous

Stop wasting money.

#IAmFabulous

NOTE TO SELF

Patience can be bitter, but her
fruit is always sweet.

#IAmFabulous

NOTE TO SELF

Stop getting distracted by things
that have nothing to do with
your goals.

#IAmFabulous

NOTE TO SELF

Enjoy the little things in life
because when you look back,
you'll see that those little
things were actually a pretty
big deal.

#IAmFabulous

NOTE TO SELF

One of the hardest battles
that you'll ever have to fight is
between who you are right now
and who you want to become.

#IAmFabulous

NOTE TO SELF

If you are NOT willing to learn,
no one can help you. If you are
determined to learn, no one can
stop you.

#IAmFabulous

NOTE TO SELF

Be selective in your battles.
Sometimes peace is better than
being right.

#IAmFabulous

NOTE TO SELF

Be Humble.
Stay faithful.
Trust God.
Trust the Process.
It all works out if you don't
give up.

#IAmFabulous

NOTE TO SELF

NEVER
NEVER
NEVER
GIVE UP.

#IAmFabulous

TRISH M MINISTRIES
Reaching The Nations

Thank you! I'm so glad that you purchased my journal.
I would love to connect with you.
Follow me on FB (Trish M Ministries),
Twitter (@LadyTrishM and Instagram (@ladytrishm).
Check out my other books that can be purchased on amazon.com:
Faith in a Barren Land
Chronicles of a Fabulous Lady
The Fabulous Wife